EXPLORING SPACE
AND BEYOND

SHUTTLE IN THE SKY

THE COLUMBIA DISASTER

by Brian Krumm

Consultant:
Steve Kortenkamp, PhD
Senior Scientist
Planetary Science Institute
Tucson, Arizona

CAPSTONE PRESS

Connect Books are published by Capstone Press,
1710 Roe Crest Drive, North Mankato, Minnesota 56003
www.capstonepub.com

This book is dedicated to the crew of the *Columbia* and their families and to all
people who risk their lives to improve life on Earth.

Library of Congress Cataloging-in-Publication Data
Krumm, Brian, author.
 Shuttle in the sky : the story of the space shuttle Columbia / by Brian Krumm.
   pages cm. — (Exploring space and beyond)
 Summary: "Describes the events before and after the Columbia disaster"—
Provided by publisher.
 Audience: Ages 8-14.
 Audience: Grades 4 to 6.
 Includes bibliographical references and index.
 ISBN 978-1-4914-4161-9 (library binding)
 ISBN 978-1-4914-4175-6 (paperback)
 ISBN 978-1-4914-4181-7 (eBook pdf)
 1. Columbia (Spacecraft)—Juvenile literature. 2. Columbia (Spacecraft)—
Accidents—Juvenile literature. 3. Space Shuttle Program (U.S.)—Juvenile
literature. 4. United States. National Aeronautics and Space Administration—
Juvenile literature. 5. Space shuttles—Accidents—United States—Juvenile
literature. 6. Outer space—Exploration—Juvenile literature. I. Title.
 TL795.515.K78 2016
 629.44'1'0973—dc23

                         2015017740

Editorial Credits
Abby Colich, editor; Kyle Grenz, designer; Wanda Winch, media researcher;
Tori Abraham, production specialist

Photo Credits
AP Photo: Dr. Scott Lieberman, 25 (bottom), Joe Cavaretta, 36, NASA TV, 18,
Terry Renna, 28; Corbis: LA Daily News/Gene Blevins, 24-25 (top); Courtesy of
Michal Kwolek, cover; Getty Images: Matt Stroshane, 29; NASA: CAIB Photo
by Rick Stiles, 2003, 35, 37, ESA/E. Olszewski (University of Arizona) - space
element, 16, 32, 35, ESA/G. Brammer, 36 (space element), ESA/Hubble Heritage
Team (StScI/AURA)/Hubble Collaboration/HST/ACS, 40-41 (space element),
Frank Michaux, 7, Jack Pfaller, 11, JPL/IPAC-Caltech, 18 (space element), JSC,
6, 10, 13, 16-17 (bottom), 20-21, 23, 38, 40, 42, 44, KSC, 4, 5, 8, 9, 14-15, 27, 33,
Nacogdoches Police Dept., 31 (top), MSFC, 43; Nova Development Corporation,
17 (top), 30-31; Shutterstock: clearviewstock, (nebula space element), Ian Doktor,
1, Melinda Fawver, binoculars

Printed in the United States of America in Stevens Point, Wisconsin
032015   008824WZF15

Table of Contents

CHAPTER 1

Liftoff!

The **space shuttle** *Columbia* shook fiercely during takeoff on January 16, 2003. The seven astronauts aboard felt their teeth chatter uncontrollably. Their bodies stayed strapped tightly to the seats. A liftoff was always a tense event. Space flight carried many risks. Mission STS-107 was no different. Even a tiny mishap could cause a huge disaster. Despite the risks, crew members were excited to spend the next several days in space.

Eight minutes after liftoff, *Columbia* was in **orbit** above Earth. It seemed that all had gone according to plan. What no one knew at the time was that a piece of foam had come off a fuel tank during takeoff. This would create a serious problem for the shuttle. It would mean that the shuttle would not survive the return to Earth.

STS stands for Space Transportation System, the space shuttle's original name.

space shuttle—a spacecraft that carries astronauts into space and back to Earth

orbit—the path an object follows as it goes around the sun or a planet

Columbia's crew, waving to onlookers on the way to Launch Pad 39A for liftoff

COLUMBIA'S CREW

Crew Member	Position	Prior Space Missions
Rick Husband	Commander	*Discovery* (1999)
Willie McCool	Pilot	first mission in space
Michael Anderson	**Payload** Commander	*Endeavour* (1998)
David Brown	Mission Specialist	first mission in space
Kalpana Chawla	Mission Specialist	*Columbia* (1997)
Laurel Clark	Mission Specialist	first mission in space
Ilan Ramon	Payload Specialist	first mission in space

payload—the items carried by a plane or other vehicle

NASA always studied the video of each liftoff. Two days after *Columbia*'s liftoff, NASA **engineers** studying the video saw a problem. They noticed a piece of foam **insulation** that broke off the main fuel tank just 81 seconds after takeoff. Foam insulation was used to keep the fuel cool. It also kept ice from building up on the shuttle.

an image captured from video, after foam debris struck the side of the shuttle

STS-107 ET208 Video
Average of 17 fields. After debris.
GMT 016:15:40:22.000 to 22.265

WHAT IS NASA?

NASA stands for National Aeronautics and Space Administration. The United States government started NASA in 1958. NASA's main job was to develop spacecraft that could travel into and explore space.

engineer—someone trained to design and build machines, vehicles, bridges, roads, or other structures

insulation—a material that stops heat, sound, or cold from entering or escaping

6

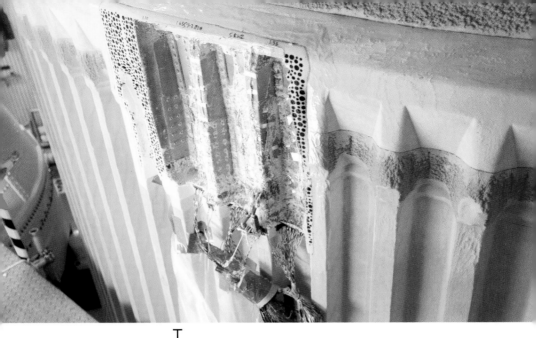

heat sensors and foam insulation

The piece of foam that broke off weighed only 1.67 pounds (0.76 kilogram). It was about the size of a suitcase. It was small and light. However, it hit the shuttle's left wing extremely hard. The incident was not unusual. Pieces of foam insulation regularly broke off during liftoff.

Engineers at NASA had been studying the foam breakoffs for years. Many of them believed foam strikes could be dangerous. If the debris hit a major part of the shuttle, it could cause serious problems.

Others at NASA downplayed the problem. They said foam strikes had not caused serious problems in the past. Therefore, there was no need to worry about them now. They didn't believe that something as light as a pillow could ever harm a spacecraft. As a result, nothing had been done to deal with the problem.

CHAPTER 2

NASA and the Shuttle Missions

NASA began the space shuttle program in the 1960s. The organization wanted to build a reusable spacecraft. Prior to the space shuttle, astronauts rode in **capsules**. The capsules traveled above powerful rockets. The rockets would separate from the capsules after takeoff. The rockets often burned up after separating. The capsules were not strong enough to be used again after returning to Earth.

By 1971 NASA had a plan. It would build a spacecraft with reusable parts. The space shuttle consisted of four main pieces. A reusable orbiter housed the crew. Two reusable rocket boosters gave the shuttle power during takeoff. The external fuel tank was the only part not reusable. It burned up in the **atmosphere** after launch.

After each mission the orbiter glided back down to Earth. It could carry up to seven astronauts. It also moved large equipment into space. Each shuttle had a lab. In this lab, astronauts performed experiments in space.

In this earlier spacecraft, *Apollo 11*, the capsule sits just below the top rocket.

capsule—a small craft that holds astronauts or other travelers

atmosphere—the mixture of gases that surrounds Earth

In 1977 NASA finished *Enterprise*, the first shuttle. To test the shuttle, *Enterprise* was flown only in Earth's atmosphere. It was not able to make further space flight. The first shuttle mission launched on April 12, 1981. The shuttle *Columbia* orbited Earth 36 times. Two days after launch, *Columbia* glided down back to Earth.

PARTS OF A SHUTTLE

external fuel tank

rocket boosters

orbiter

Early missions had focused on space exploration. *Columbia*'s 2003 mission, however, was focused mainly on scientific experiments for research.

Some people later used the mission to argue against the shuttle program. They said shuttle flights were not worth the danger to astronauts. In addition, each mission cost millions of dollars. People objected to any mission that wasn't absolutely necessary. They thought the money should be used for other programs.

Astronaut Michael Anderson reads a checklist.

Columbia's crew completed more than 80 scientific experiments while in space. Some experiments involved studying the effects of **microgravity** on animals and insects. Bees, ants, spiders, silkworms, cocoons, fish, and rats were also aboard *Columbia*. The crew also studied pollution. They observed the dust in Earth's atmosphere. Astronauts tested how their own bodies reacted to being in space. They also studied the growth of cancer cells. They hoped the research could help find a cure.

THERMAL PROTECTION SYSTEM

Spacecraft are exposed to extreme hot and cold during space travel. *Columbia*, like the other shuttles, was protected from these temperatures by the thermal protection system (TPS). A layer of lightweight tiles covered the orbiter. Without the TPS, the orbiter would not survive its return to Earth. However, the TPS could easily be damaged. When the foam hit *Columbia*'s left wing during liftoff, it harmed one of the TPS tiles. This allowed hot gases to leak into the left wing during reentry.

close-up of the thermal protection system tiles protecting the cockpit

microgravity—the condition of weightlessness in space

Friday, January 31, 2003, was *Columbia*'s last full day in space. The crew began planning for return to Earth. The first step was to bring the shuttle back into Earth's atmosphere. The process was called reentry. Before reentry, many preparations took place. Some astronauts took turns practicing landing the shuttle with a computer. Others made sure the experiments were complete. They were excited about the results of their research.

Payload Commander Michael Anderson sent a message from space. "It's kind of with mixed emotions as we get ready to come home, but we have enough fond memories to last us for a lifetime."

Fact

The astronauts sent the findings of their experiments to NASA from space. The results of their work were not lost in the accident.

"NO CONCERN"

NASA informed the *Columbia* crew about the foam strike during flight. At the time, NASA did not know the great damage done to the shuttle. NASA workers sent an email to astronauts on the shuttle. It said, "This item is not worth mentioning other than so you're not surprised by it in a question from a reporter.... There is absolutely no concern for entry."

clockwise from top right, *Columbia* crew members: Ilan Ramon, David Brown, Michael Anderson, and Kalpana Chawla

CHAPTER 3

Eyes on the Sky

Back on Earth space enthusiasts waited to watch the shuttle make its reentry. Family members of the crew eagerly waited for *Columbia* to return. NASA workers prepared for the shuttle's landing. Some spectators around the country prepared to film the shuttle's return. Others watched through powerful telescopes.

At the Kennedy Space Center near Cape Canaveral, Florida, many people arrived shortly after sunrise on February 1, 2003. They were expecting to see the shuttle touch down on the landing strip and glide to a stop.

About 120 NASA workers, reporters, and guests sat on bleachers near the landing strip. On a separate set of bleachers, the families of the crew also waited. A former astronaut sat with each family. They were there to answer any questions family members might have.

Columbia was due to land on this runway on February 1, 2003.

Media interest in shuttle landings had not been as high as in years prior. However, a group of reporters had still gathered at the viewing site. Reporter William Harwood was preparing a news story on the mission. He planned to publish it on the Internet the minute that *Columbia* touched down.

Photographer Gene Blevins had set up cameras near Bishop, California. He planned to film the shuttle's reentry. "Sure enough … here comes this big white dot out over the mountains coming right at us. This thing was coming at incredible speed," Blevins later said.

FLIGHT DIRECTO

NASA workers at **mission control** in Houston, Texas, got ready for the landing. They studied the weather conditions and went over final details. Entry Flight Director LeRoy Cain was preparing to help guide *Columbia* to a safe landing. His job was to direct the shuttle's return to Earth.

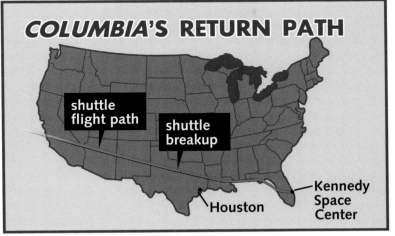

COLUMBIA'S RETURN PATH

shuttle flight path

shuttle breakup

Houston

Kennedy Space Center

mission control—the group that manages space flight from takeoff until landing

Columbia Flight Directors LeRoy Cain (left) and Steve Stich

Onboard the shuttle, crew members were laughing and enjoying themselves. They were anxious but excited to return home. Each crew member performed his or her assigned tasks. None of them noticed anything unusual. Pilot Willie McCool watched the shuttle glow in the extreme heat outside.

"Looks like a blast furnace ... it's really getting bright out there," he said.

Commander Rick Husband replied, "Yeah, you definitely don't want to be out there now."

McCool and Husband were talking about just how hot the atmosphere is during reentry. At 2,000° Fahrenheit (1,093° Celsius), it's about five times hotter than cookies baking in an oven.

The shuttle traveled at 17,000 miles (27,000 km) per hour. It flew 40 miles (64 km) above Earth. The crew was unaware that very hot gases had started to enter *Columbia*'s left wing. This was where the foam had struck. Mission control would soon see the first signs of trouble.

crew members prepare for reentry

CHAPTER 4

Disaster Strikes

At about 8:50 a.m., mission control worker Jeff Kling noticed something unusual on a **monitor**. Four of the temperature **sensors** on the left wing of the shuttle had suddenly stopped working. All other systems appeared normal. Seconds later, *Columbia*'s commander, Rick Husband, contacted mission control.

"We just lost tire pressure on ... both tires," Husband said. Then Husband said something that mission control couldn't understand. The signal had become choppy.

shuttle flight control room in Houston's Mission Control Center at NASA's Johnson Space Center

monitor—a video screen used for display

sensor—an instrument that detects changes and sends information to a controlling device

Another worker in Houston, Charles Hobaugh, radioed *Columbia*. "And *Columbia*, Houston, we see your tire pressure messages," he said, "and we did not copy your last."

Husband made another attempt to contact mission control. He couldn't get through. The connection was lost. At the exact same time, all data that had been flowing from the shuttle to mission control suddenly stopped.

In Florida the spectators and family members had no idea what was unfolding at mission control. But a few reporters had noticed something strange. A TV in a NASA building near the runway had been showing *Columbia*'s progress on a map. A glowing red triangle that had been marking the location of *Columbia* had stopped moving.

At mission control Hobaugh tried to make contact with *Columbia*'s crew. But there was no reply.

Hobaugh tried again at 9:03 a.m., saying, "Columbia, Houston, comm check." But he was met with silence.

Charles Hobaugh attempted the final radio communications with *Columbia*.

In California photographer Gene Blevins, looking through his camera lens, noticed that something was wrong. Turning to another photographer, he said, "Did you see that? Something just came off the shuttle!" The shuttle had begun to break up into smaller and smaller pieces, leaving streaks of light in its path.

A spectator in Texas sent William Harwood, a reporter in Florida, a text message. It read, "The shuttle broke up!" When Harwood read the message, he felt a chill come over him.

Columbia breaks up leaving a trail of debris in this photo over Tyler, Texas, shot by Scott Lieberman.

On the ground onlookers could see what was happening as they gazed at the sky. People in Texas, Arkansas, and Louisiana made several calls to 911. They reported loud noises and lights in the sky. The lights could be seen without a telescope. These people were witnessing the *Columbia* breaking into pieces in the morning sky.

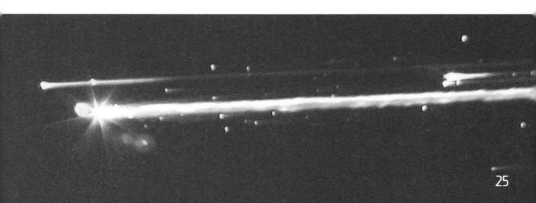

Back at mission control, Entry Flight Director LeRoy Cain ordered the doors to be locked. "No phone calls out of this room," he said. "No data transmissions anywhere." He was taking the first steps of NASA's emergency plan. The plan had only been used once before—when the shuttle *Challenger* exploded in 1986.

"I knew that the vehicle had broken up over Texas," Cain later said. "You just go into a mode of capturing all notes and data." Cain started leading everyone through the emergency plan checklist. The checklist detailed the steps to take after an emergency. It was a checklist mission control hoped to never use again.

At Kennedy Space Center, the families of the astronauts were rushed into a building reserved for crew members. There they were told the devastating news. Rona Ramon, wife of astronaut Ilan Ramon, was absolutely shocked. "I just looked up at the sky and said, 'God, bring him back to me.'"

Engine exhaust, smoke plumes, and an expanding ball of gas marked the scene of the *Challenger* disaster in 1986.

CHALLENGER DISASTER

On January 28, 1986, the space shuttle *Challenger* broke apart about 70 seconds after liftoff. Three towers of fiery smoke hung in the air. Stunned spectators stared into the sky. A part called an O-ring in a rocket booster failed during liftoff. Cold weather that day was the cause. All seven crew members aboard died. Space shuttle flights were stopped for the next 32 months. During this time, NASA redesigned some shuttle parts and made other changes. People were confident a tragedy like this would never happen again. The *Columbia* disaster proved them wrong.

All around the world, people were shocked. For those who had been alive during the *Challenger* disaster, February 1 brought back painful memories. It was also a reminder of just how dangerous space exploration can be.

President George W. Bush publicly addressed the nation concerning the tragedy later that afternoon.

"This day has brought terrible news and great sadness to our country ..." Bush said. "The *Columbia* is lost; there are no survivors." Bush expressed sorrow for the families of the astronauts. He pledged that the U.S. space program would continue. "Our journey into space will go on," he stated.

Spectators at Kennedy Space Center in Florida were shocked after the *Columbia* disaster.

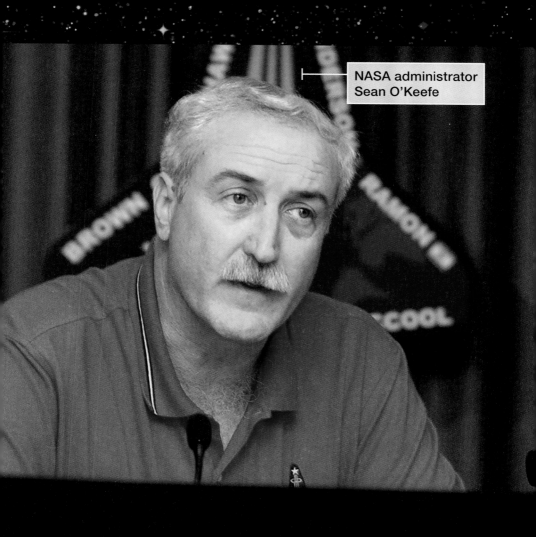

NASA administrator
Sean O'Keefe

NASA held a press conference that same day.
NASA **administrator** Sean O'Keefe said, "This
is indeed a tragic day for the NASA family, for the
families of the astronauts who flew on STS-107,
and likewise is tragic for the nation."

administrator—a person who directs a business or
other organization

29

CHAPTER 5

Finding the Cause

NASA continued to follow the steps in its emergency plan. The same day the shuttle broke apart, NASA set up a board to investigate the disaster.

NASA quickly determined there could be no survivors. One of the board's first tasks was to search for human remains. They would also search for the shuttle wreckage. These tasks would not be easy. The shuttle had broken up over an area that ranged from western Louisiana to central Texas. There were 500 square miles (800 square km) to cover.

Scott Hubbard, a member of the board, later recalled his feelings when the investigation began. "It was a very emotional time.... You really felt a sense of loss."

board—a group of people who manage, direct, or investigate

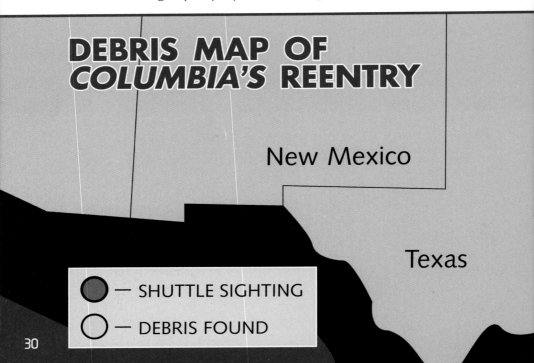

DEBRIS MAP OF COLUMBIA'S REENTRY

New Mexico

Texas

○ — SHUTTLE SIGHTING

○ — DEBRIS FOUND

Search and rescue teams set out right away. About 20,000 volunteers searched the wreckage area. Thousands of the searchers were wilderness firefighters. They came from all over the United States. More than 80,000 pieces of the shuttle were found. Hundreds of citizens discovered pieces of the wreckage. They reported the locations to NASA officials. This aided the volunteers in their recovery efforts. However, many reports of debris findings turned out to be unrelated to *Columbia*.

Fact

In 2011 a large chemical tank from *Columbia* was discovered in a lake about 160 miles (258 km) northeast of Houston. It had been there ever since the disaster eight years earlier. A drought in 2011 dried up the lake and exposed the tank.

a map of shuttle sightings (yellow) and debris findings (red)

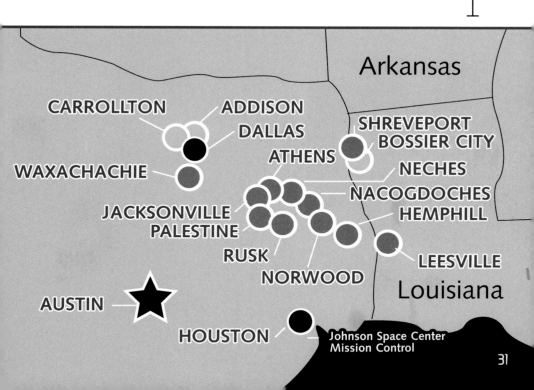

Arkansas

CARROLLTON   ADDISON
             DALLAS
             ATHENS
WAXACHACHIE

SHREVEPORT
BOSSIER CITY
NECHES
NACOGDOCHES
HEMPHILL

JACKSONVILLE
PALESTINE
RUSK
NORWOOD

LEESVILLE

Louisiana

AUSTIN

HOUSTON   Johnson Space Center
          Mission Control

Teams at NASA studied the wreckage. They laid out the pieces in the shape of the shuttle. They matched each piece to where it originally belonged on *Columbia*. Clues from the wreckage pointed to a likely cause. There was damage to the shuttle's left wing. Engineers remembered the foam strike during liftoff. They brought this up again. Some at NASA still didn't believe that a piece of foam could have damaged the shuttle so badly.

The *Columbia* Reconstruction Project Team collected shuttle debris.

The wreckage from *Columbia* is now stored at Kennedy Space Center. The media were invited just once to view the 84,000 pieces of debris. Now only researchers are allowed in the room where the debris is kept.

Members of the media also doubted the foam harmed the shuttle. Board member Scott Hubbard remembered the reaction to this idea: "We had people in the shuttle program saying, 'Oh, these guys are "foamologists!"' They would hold a piece of foam up on national TV and ask, 'How could anything this light do any damage?'"

Members of the board made some calculations. They said the foam that broke off was likely traveling at 500 miles (800 km) per hour. This means the foam hit the shuttle with tremendous force.

More efforts were made to show the harm the foam had caused. Hubbard had a team build an exact copy of the shuttle's wing. The team used the same materials that *Columbia* was made from. An outdoor test was held on May 14, 2003, in San Antonio, Texas. TV crews, scientists, and some family members of *Columbia*'s crew were present.

In the test, a large air gun fired a piece of foam at the model wing. The foam was the same size as the piece that hit *Columbia*. A wide hole was left in the wing. Hubbard and his team had shown the damage the foam strike caused during *Columbia*'s liftoff.

an experiment showing the impact of foam on shuttle materials

The board issued a final report on the *Columbia* disaster on August 26, 2003. The problem with pieces of foam falling off the shuttle had been known for years. Why hadn't the problem been fixed? The report criticized NASA for not solving the foam problem. It also pointed out other problems at NASA.

The report stated that "practices [harmful] to safety were allowed to develop." It also said that NASA put too much faith in past successes. This kept NASA workers from paying enough attention to possible danger. The report also said that NASA did not have enough funding and worked under too tight of a schedule.

a piece of foam, displayed by Program Manager Ron Dittemore

The *Columbia* Accident Investigation Board speaks to reporters.

The report said that NASA needed to search for and fix all safety problems. Better cameras needed to be attached to space shuttles. This would allow NASA to see more damage during liftoff. The report added that equipment needed updating and that space shuttles should eventually be replaced with more modern space vehicles.

the space shuttle *Atlantis*

NASA administrator Sean O'Keefe responded to the report.

"We have accepted the findings," he said. He stated that NASA "will comply with the recommendations to the best of our ability.... The board has provided NASA with an important road map as we determine when we will be 'fit to fly' again."

Harold Gehman, **chairman** of the board, said that NASA "is not capable of safely operating the shuttle over the long term. That's the bottom line."

The shuttle program was stopped for two years. During this time NASA redesigned the external fuel tank. It became much safer. NASA also updated other equipment and developed new safety procedures.

RESCUE MISSION

During its investigation, the board asked scientists if *Columbia*'s crew could have been rescued. They said it would have been possible while the space shuttle was still in orbit. The space shuttle *Atlantis* was due to launch soon after *Columbia*'s return. *Atlantis* could have been prepared for an early liftoff. In space *Columbia*'s crew could have moved onto *Atlantis*. While this plan was not impossible, it would have been very difficult. It also would have been very dangerous. NASA would have had to skip several steps in preparing *Atlantis* for flight. There also could have been danger to *Atlantis*' crew.

chairman—a person of authority

Astronaut Eileen Collins reads a checklist in *Discovery*'s cabin.

The report made an impact. President Bush said in 2004 that the space shuttle program would end within the next few years. The remaining shuttles would be retired after completion of the **International Space Station**. Later in 2004, Bush and NASA told of a new plan. NASA would replace the shuttle. The new spacecraft could take astronauts to the moon, to Mars, and beyond.

"We do not know where this journey will end," Bush said, "yet we know this: Human beings are headed into the cosmos."

In July 2005 the space shuttle *Discovery* lifted off on mission STS-114. This was the first mission after the *Columbia* disaster. *Discovery*'s crew tested new safety methods. Astronauts used cameras and a robotic arm to check the shuttle for damage. NASA also used more cameras to check the foam insulation during liftoff.

Commander Eileen Collins sent a message to mission control. "We reflect on the last shuttle mission—the great ship *Columbia*—and her ... crew: Rick, Willie, Mike, KC, Dave, Laurel, and Ilan. We miss them and we are continuing their mission. God bless them and God bless their families."

International Space Station—a place for astronauts to live and work in space

CHAPTER 6

Beyond the Shuttle

The space shuttle program continued for six more years. *Atlantis* rolled to a stop at Kennedy Space Center on July 21, 2011, ending the final shuttle mission. The shuttle took about 10,000 pounds (4,500 kg) of spare parts to the International Space Station. It also delivered about 3,000 pounds (1,400 kg) of food. It brought about 6,000 pounds (2,700 kg) of unneeded supplies back to Earth. This final mission brought to a close 30 years of space shuttle flights.

The final space shuttle mission ended with the landing of *Atlantis.*

In 2014 NASA began developing the Space Launch System (SLS). The SLS is the first spacecraft since the shuttle that can take astronauts to space. It will be the most powerful spacecraft ever built. It will allow astronauts to land on Mars, **asteroids**, and other objects in space.

The first mission is set to lift off in 2018. A capsule will travel around the moon and back. If all goes as planned, NASA could send humans to Mars by the year 2032. Without the contributions and sacrifices of earlier astronauts, such as the men and women of *Columbia*, this exploration might have never been possible.

artist rendering of NASA's Space Launch System

asteroid—a large rock that travels through space

Timeline of *Columbia's* Flight

January 16, 2003

The space shuttle *Columbia* blasts off on mission STS-107. A few moments later, a piece of foam insulation from a fuel tank breaks off. The foam hits the shuttle's left wing with extreme force.

January 23, 2003

NASA sends an email to the crew aboard *Columbia* telling them about the foam strike. The email says there is "no concern" for reentry or damage to the shuttle.

January 31, 2003

Columbia's crew has finished all assigned research projects. They finalize the data and being preparations for reentry.

February 1, 2003

8:15 a.m.
Columbia fires braking rockets as it soars toward a planned touchdown at Kennedy Space Center, Runway 33, in Cape Canaveral, Florida.

8:53 a.m.
Ground controllers at NASA's Mission Control lose temperature data for the shuttle's left hydraulic system. Crew members are not alerted about the situation.

8:58 a.m.
Flow of data from temperature sensors on the shuttle's left wing is lost.

8:59 a.m.
Flow of data is lost from temperature and tire pressure sensors on the shuttle's left side. Crew members are alerted about the data loss.

9:00 a.m.
Mission Control suddenly loses all contact with *Columbia*. People in Texas, Arkansas, and Louisiana report hearing explosions and seeing flaming debris in the sky.

9:16 a.m.
NASA contacts U.S. President George W. Bush and reports on the possible disaster.

9:29 a.m.
NASA declares an emergency.

9:44 a.m.
NASA warns disaster witnesses and people close to shuttle's flight plan to stay away from dangerous debris.

11:00 a.m.
NASA lowers the U.S. flag next to its countdown clock at Kennedy Space Center to half-staff, indicating a national disaster.

1:00 p.m.
NASA officially announces that all aboard *Columbia* have died.

2:00 p.m.
President Bush addresses a mourning United States and acknowledges the loss of *Columbia*, offering condolences for the families of the crew.

August 26, 2003

The *Columbia* Accident Investigation Board releases its final report. The report concludes that the foam strike led to the break up of *Columbia*. It also states that NASA must make future space flight safer.

Glossary

administrator (add-MIN-uh-strait-uhr)—a person who directs a business or other organization

asteroid (AS-tuh-royd)—a large rock that travels through space

atmosphere (AT-muhss-fihr)—the mixture of gases that surrounds Earth

board (BORD)—a group of people who manage, direct, or investigate

capsule (KAP-suhl)—a small craft that holds astronauts or other travelers

chairman (CHAIR-man)—a person of authority

engineer (en-juh-NEER)—someone trained to design and build machines, vehicles, bridges, roads, or other structures

insulation (in-suh-LAY-shun)—a material that stops heat, sound, or cold from entering or escaping

International Space Station (in-tur-NASH-uh-nuhl SPAYSS STAY-shuhn)—a place for astronauts to live and work in space

microgravity (mye-kruh-GRAV-uh-tee)—the condition of weightlessness in space

mission control (MISH-uhn kuhn-TROHL)—the group that manages space flight from takeoff until landing

monitor (MON-uh-tur)—a video screen used for display

orbit (OR-bit)—the path an object follows as it goes around the sun or a planet

payload (PAY-lohd)—the items carried by a plane or other vehicle

sensor (SEN-sur)—an instrument that detects changes and sends information to a controlling device

space shuttle (SPAYSS SHUHT-uhl)—a spacecraft that carries astronauts into space and back to Earth

Critical Thinking Using the Common Core

1. Reread the text on pages 8–9 and study the photographs. What is similar and different about each type of spacecraft? Why might one have been more efficient than the other? (Craft and Structure)

2. What is the purpose of NASA and the shuttle missions? How was this *Columbia* mission trying to help those on Earth while in space? (Key Idea and Details)

3. What might be different if NASA had addressed the issues with foam falling off the shuttles? Do you think the rescue mission described on page 39 could have been successful? Why or why not? (Integration of Knowledge and Ideas)

Read More

Jennings, Ken. *Outer Space.* Junior Genius Guides. New York: Little Simon, 2015.

Sexton, Colleen. *Space Shuttles. Blastoff!* Readers: Exploring Space. Minneapolis: Bellweather Media, 2010.

Wallace, Karen. *Rockets and Spaceships.* New York: DK Publishing, 2011.

Internet Sites

FactHound offers a safe, fun way to find Internet sites related to this book. All of the sites on FactHound have been researched by our staff.

Here's all you do:

Visit *www.facthound.com*

Type in this code: 978149441619

Check out projects, games and lots more at
www.capstonekids.com

Index